The Pleistocene Era: The History of the Ice Age and the Dawn of Modern Humans

By Charles River Editors

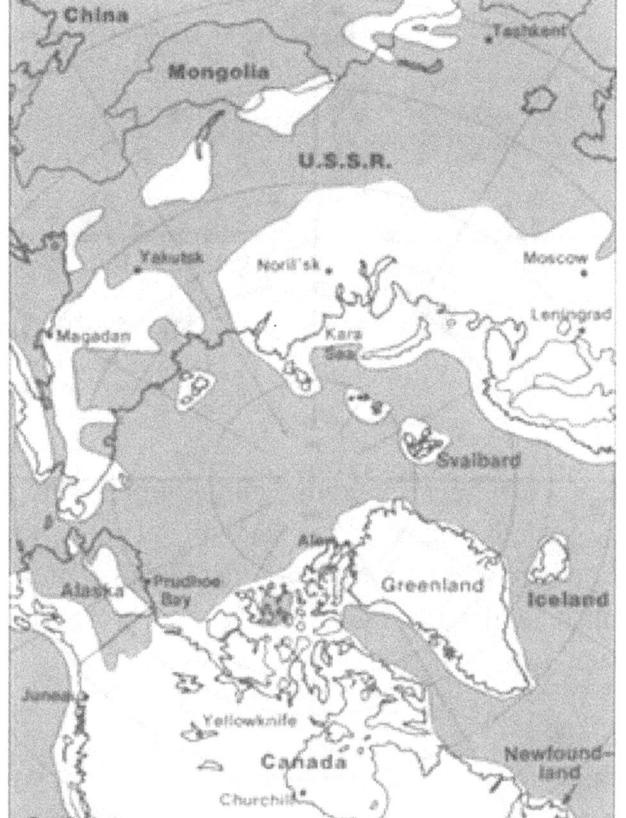

A map of ice extension across the north pole during the Pleistocene

About Charles River Editors

Charles River Editors provides superior editing and original writing services across the digital publishing industry, with the expertise to create digital content for publishers across a vast range of subject matter. In addition to providing original digital content for third party publishers, we also republish civilization's greatest literary works, bringing them to new generations of readers via ebooks.

Sign up here to receive updates about free books as we publish them, and visit Our Kindle Author Page to browse today's free promotions and our most recently published Kindle titles.

Introduction

A depiction of various forms of life during the Pleistocene

The early history of Earth covers such vast stretches of time that years, centuries, and even millennia become virtually meaningless. Instead, paleontologists and scientists who study geochronology divide time into periods and eras.

The current view of science is that Earth is around 4.6 billion years old, and the first 4 billion years of its development are known as the Precambrian period. For the first billion years or so, there was no life in Earth. Then the first single-celled life-forms, early bacteria and algae, began to emerge. It's unclear where they came from or even if they originated on this planet at all, but this gradual development continued until around 4 billion years ago when suddenly (in geological terms) more complex forms of life began to emerge. Scientists call this time of an explosion of new forms of life the Paleozoic Era, and it stretched from around 541-250 million years ago (mya). In the oceans and then on land, new creatures and plants began to appear in bewildering variety, and by the end of this period, life on Earth had diversified into a myriad of complex forms that filled virtually every habitat and niche available in the seas and on the planet's only continent, Pangea.

The Pleistocene spans a period from around 2.5 mya to just over 12,000 years ago, and it was an epoch of enormous change on Earth, mainly characterized by climate changes involving fluctuations between periods of extreme heat and long periods of glaciation. This period is commonly known as the Ice Age despite the fact there were actually a number of separate periods of cold.

Along with the climate challenges, this was also the period that saw the development of modern humans. The origin of our ancient ancestors is still a matter of debate amongst paleontologists, and classification systems for early hominoids are constantly being updated as new discoveries are made. What is generally agreed upon is the species *Homo sapiens* belong to the order primates and the sub-order anthropoids. Within the anthropoids sub-order, humans belong to the family hominids, which also includes other animals such as the orangutan and the great apes. Drilling down even further, humans belong to a sub-group of hominids known as hominin. The sub-group hominin includes humans, as well as chimpanzees and gorillas.

Discoveries have revealed more than twenty species of the genus *Homo*, all of which appeared during the Pleistocene Epoch, and all but *Homo sapiens* became extinct during the same period. The challenge is understanding which of these groups are predecessors to *Homo sapiens* and which are separate groups that died out leaving no current representation. Not knowing this information makes it difficult to determine neat classification and establish precisely when hominins separated from the rest of the non-hominin primates.

It is generally accepted that hominoids and the first hominins evolved in what is now Africa. Somewhere around 7 mya, the common hominoid lineage split into two distinct evolutionary lines: the ancestors of modern chimpanzees and those of modern humans. Around 2.5 mya, a new genus of hominin appeared. *Homo* had larger brains than their predecessors as well as smaller jaws and teeth. The very first stone tools date to this period when there were a number of different hominin species. The very first true humans, *Homo erectus*, appeared around 2 mya.

These new creatures could hardly have chosen a more difficult time to appear. In addition to facing the challenges of simply surviving in a generally hostile environment, the world was about to enter a period of convulsive climatic change. The new humans would face drought and extreme heat, as well as long periods of cooling where glaciers spread across the surface of the planet, but they survived, and by the time the Pleistocene Epoch ended around 12,000 years ago, *Homo sapiens* had become one of the most significant species on the planet.

The Pleistocene Era: The History of the Ice Age and the Dawn of Modern Humans looks at the development of the era, what life on Earth was like, and the origins of archaic humans. Along with pictures depicting important people, places, and events, you will learn about the Pleistocene like never before.

Background

The modern understanding of the creation and development of planet Earth really began to emerge in the early 19th century when geologists first began to analyze rock strata and to recognize that different layers contained different kinds of fossil remains. It was quickly realized that these provided a snapshot of life at various periods in the ancient past and it didn't take long before scientists began to use agreed terms to describe the vast stretches of time that comprise the history of our planet.

One of the first was a self-taught English geologist named John Phillips and in the 1830s he published a book that would change our understanding of the history of the planet and finally standardize the terminology used to describe these ancient periods. He did this by ordering rock strata according to the different types of fossils found within them and used this to define different periods of the development of life on Earth.

Phillips

These classifications describe the history of life after the Precambrian period in terms of three eras, with each being further subdivided into several periods. These eras are:

The Paleozoic Era (meaning the era of "ancient life") was the oldest and a period of dramatic upheaval and change. It covers a period from 550-250 mya. This era began with the emergence of the first multi-celled life and by its end, the first large reptiles, creatures such as Dimetrodon and Edaphosaurus, had appeared on the single continent, Pangea. This era is further subdivided into six geologic periods; Cambrian, Ordovician, Silurian, Devonian, Carboniferous and Permian.

The Paleozoic Era was generally a period of unbroken evolution of increasingly complex forms of life. However, it also included at least three of what have become known as "mass extinction events." For reasons that are not fully understood but are most likely associated with some form of climate change, there were three occasions during this era when many species completely died and were replaced by other forms of life.

The first of these events occurred between the Ordovician and Silurian periods. The Earth grew colder, glaciers appeared and sea levels and sea temperatures dropped dramatically. Around 25% of all species on Earth were killed. In the oceans the effect was even more dramatic and around 60% of all marine species vanished forever.

At the end of the Devonian period there was a second and even more catastrophic extinction event that led to the death of around 70% of all species on Earth. No-one is quite certain what caused this event though current theories include excessive sedimentation of the oceans, a period of rapid global warming (or cooling), the impact of a comet or large meteorite or even habitat changes caused by massive nutrient runoff from the land.

Then, at the end of the Permian period there was an extinction event so cataclysmic that it became known to early paleontologists as "the great dying." In a period that may have been a short as twenty thousand years, 95% of all species of animal were wiped out and virtually all trees and many plants disappeared. Just like other extinction events, no-one is entirely sure what caused the great dying, but recent discoveries may give a strong clue.

Rocks in present-day Australia and Antarctica have been discovered that contain tiny quartz crystals marked with microscopic fractures. Quartz is incredibly strong and it would take enormous force to do this, many times the power of a nuclear explosion. It is thought that perhaps a huge asteroid more than three miles (4.8 kilometers) in diameter may have struck the Earth causing a sudden and cataclysmic change in climate.

Clouds of particles and gases would have blocked out the sun for months or perhaps even years. Global temperatures would have initially dropped and corrosive rain and snow would have begun to fall. When this eventually stopped, the atmosphere would have been filled with greenhouse gases and a period of global warming would have followed that may have lasted for millions of years. Earth became a blank slate, ready for entirely new forms of life to appear.

The next era was the Mesozoic Era (meaning the era of "middle life"), spanning a period from around 250-66 million years ago. Like the previous era, this was a period of continual change. It was also the period when large reptiles first began to appear and then became the dominant form of life on Earth. This era is subdivided into three geologic periods; Triassic, Jurassic and Cretaceous.

The Triassic period saw new forms of life appear on Earth to replace those killed during the Permian extinction. The first true dinosaurs began to appear, though they were much smaller than those that followed, and these spread out across the single continent, Pangea. However, towards the end of the Triassic period there was yet another global mass-extinction that saw around 35% of all species being killed. Paleontologists are not certain what caused this event but, like earlier mass-extinctions, it is thought to have been caused by some form of climatic change.

The most prevalent theory is that there was a period of large-scale release of greenhouse gases into the atmosphere, perhaps caused by widespread volcanic activity. This is thought to have caused widespread global warming and the acidification of the oceans. The rise in temperature caused the extinction of many species, but one type of creature seems to have been virtually unaffected: reptiles. Perhaps the cold-blooded reptiles were better able to survive rising temperatures? No-one is certain, but we do now that at the end of the Triassic period, the extinction of many other species left reptiles able to proliferate and expand to fill virtually every evolutionary niche.

The following Jurassic period saw the beginning of complete reptile dominance of the planet. Huge herds of sauropods roamed Pangea's fern-covered interior, hunted by predators such as Allosaurus. In the Oceans, mighty marine reptiles, the Mosasaurs, hunted fish and other sea creatures. Flying reptiles, pterosaurs, dominated the skies. By the end of the Jurassic period, dinosaurs were the most successful and diverse form of life on earth. In the period that followed, the Cretaceous, they would become even more abundant, diverse and specialized.

There are no precise dates associated with the Jurassic period. The spans of time involved are so vast that all we have are vague approximations. For example, the end of the Triassic period and the global extinction event that followed may have covered a period of twenty thousand years. Or two hundred thousand. Or two million years. Each has been suggested and each has been accepted (and rejected) by some paleontologists. The date given for the end of the Jurassic period varies by as much as five million years according to different theories. It is important to remember that we are not dealing here with the kind of precise dates that characterize human history. The early history of planet Earth proceeded in a relatively leisurely way, with events unfolding over millions of years. The periods and dates we are dealing with here are neither fixed nor generally agreed with absolute certainty.

The most recent chapter in the history of the planet, and the one that modern societies live in today, is the Cenozoic Era, the era of "new life."

The following is the list of geological periods and the range of ages in millions of years ago (mya) to hundreds of thousands of years ago (kya):

- Precambrian - 4,600–541 mya

- Cambrian - 541–485.4 mya

- Ordovician - 485.4–443.8 mya - Ending with first major extinction.

- Silurian - 443.8–419.2 mya

- Devonian - 419.2–358.9 mya - Ending with second major extinction.

- Carboniferous - 358.9–298.9 mya

- Permian - - 298.9–251.902 mya - Ending with third major extinction.

- Triassic - 251.9–201.3 mya - Ending with fourth major extinction.

- Jurassic - 201.3–145 mya

- Cretaceous - 145–66 mya - Ending with fifth major extinction.

- Paleogene - 66–23.03 mya

- Neogene - 23.03–2.58 mya

- Quaternary - 2.58 mya to Present

The Quaternary Period is the shortest period in the eon, covering a little more than two and a half million years. This period is further divided into two epochs, the Pleistocene (2.58 mya – 11.7 kya) and the Holocene (11.7 kya to the present). The Pleistocene Epoch is further divided into four ages: the Gelasian (2.58 – 1.8 mya); the Calabrian (1.8 mya – 774 kya); the Ionian, also known as the Chibanian or Middle (774 -129 kya); and the Tarantian, also known as the Upper (129 kya – 11.7 kya).

The names given to periods and epochs clearly reflect early paleontologists' attempts to understand the geological history of Earth. Immediately before the Pleistocene Epoch was the Pliocene Epoch, the last epoch of the Neogene Period. Pliocene is a Latin word meaning *newer* because when this epoch was named, it was considered to be the most recent period, but in the 19th century, Scottish geologist Sir Charles Lyell proposed another classification. He noted that more than 70% of mollusk fossils from around 2.5 mya were of creatures that still existed, and he suggested the name Pleistocene for the new epoch, another Latin term meaning "newest." This new classification was generally accepted until the consensus was reached that the period from the end of widespread glaciation around 12,000 years ago should be identified as a separate epoch. This led to the naming of the Holocene Epoch, meaning "wholly new." In other words, there are three consecutive geological timespans with names meaning newer, newest, and wholly new.

These timespans are purely geological classifications with divisions between periods mainly characterized by the appearance - or disappearance - of particular types of fossil. However, anthropologists, those who study the history and science of the human race, use quite different classifications. For anthropologists, the period extending from the earliest known use of stone tools (around 3.3 mya) to the end of the Pleistocene Epoch (11.7 kya) is called the Paleolithic period, also known as the Stone Age. This means a study of the Pleistocene Epoch also covers the majority of the Paleolithic period. Furthermore, a discussion of the changes the planet went through during this period is also the story of how the human race adapted and evolved into the earliest recognizable human societies.

The Geology and Climate of the Pleistocene Period

More is known about the history of the Pleistocene Epoch than any other period simply because it is one of the most recent geological periods. While each new layer of sedimentation and erosion typically obliterates at least part of what has gone before, this has not happened in the case of the Pleistocene period. As G.K. Gilbert put it, "When the work of the geologist is finished and his final comprehensive report written, the longest and most important chapter will be upon the latest and shortest of the geologic periods. The chapter will be longest because the exceptional fullness of the record of the latest period will enable him to set forth most completely its complex history."[1]

The timespan of the Pleistocene Epoch may be comparatively short, but it is also extremely complex and leaves open to debate a number of important questions. The Gelasian Age (2.5 to 1.8 mya) was originally classified as part of the Pliocene Epoch, which took place just before the Pleistocene Epoch. However, as recently as 1998, the Gelasian Age was instead included in the Pleistocene Epoch. This change was mainly to more closely correlate geologic periods to major changes in the Earth's climate. The name Gelasian comes from the city of Gela in Sicily where many early finds relating to this period were discovered.

Unlike previous periods, the Pleistocene Epoch is not known for large geological upheavals or major changes on the Earth's surface. When this period began, the continents were likely close to their current positions. Most estimates suggest that they have moved less than 100 kilometers from the beginning of the Pleistocene Epoch to the present. Perhaps the most notable difference in the continents between the Pleistocene and today was the disconnection of continents caused by higher sea levels during periods of glaciation. For example, during much of the Pleistocene,

---

[1] Gilbert, G. K., *Lake Bonneville*, 1890, U. S. Geological Survey.

what is now Siberia was connected to Alaska by the Bering Land Bridge, an open steppe. Also, it would have been possible to walk from what is now New Guinea to mainland Australia. As sea levels rose during interglacial periods, these bridges were covered by the ocean, separating North America from Eurasia and Australia from New Guinea.

Although the geology of this period may have been relatively quiet, the climate was the precise opposite. Climate change is a subject of surpassing interest and heated debate today, but during the Pleistocene Epoch the climate went through a series of convulsions unlike anything seen before. The Calabrian Age (1.8 mya – 774 kya) saw a number of cold/warm cycles. Discoveries in Europe suggest a minimum of five periglacial periods where the climate was sufficiently cold to produce permafrost, but there were not the massive glaciers that accompanied later cold periods. Each of the cold cycles created subarctic conditions in western Europe and Arctic steppes in east-central Europe.

During the Middle and Upper Pleistocene (1.8 mya – around 12 kya) there were a number of additional cold/warm cycles. The precise number of these cycles is difficult to define, but most areas of Europe, for example, were subject to between five and eight periods of intense cold. Deep-sea cores taken in the Atlantic and Pacific Oceans reflect a similar number of periods of extreme cold, suggesting that these temperature fluctuations were a global phenomenon.

These later fluctuations brought glaciers south from the ice caps. It has been estimated that Arctic glaciers may have extended as far south as southern Europe and the Mediterranean Sea. As much as 30% of Earth's surface may have been covered by vast ice sheets. The Cordilleran ice sheet blanketed much of the northwest of what is now North America while the Fenno-Scandian ice sheet covered northern Europe, including the Alps. All the northern seas were covered by sheets of ice. Beyond the glaciers themselves, an area of permafrost extended far beyond. Interspersing these cold periods were times where the climate was much warmer, very similar to today's climate. These cold and warm periods are generally known as glacial and interglacial periods.

The peak of the last and most intense period of cold occurred around 18,000 years ago. Some scientists believe that these periods of intense cold have not ended, and that we are currently living in an interglacial period that has lasted for more than ten thousand years.

There has been a great deal of debate about precisely what caused these temperature fluctuations. These are not confined to the Pleistocene, but they do seem to have been more frequent during that epoch. It has been calculated that from 2.8 mya – 12 kya, there may have been up to twenty-five separate advances and retreats of ice sheets. One of the questions that continues to perplex scientists is precisely what caused these changes? Advances in astronomy may help to provide at least part of the answer.

It is now known that the Earth does not orbit smoothly and regularly around the sun. The Earth's orbit is eccentric, meaning Earth's orbit is nearly circular around the sun. It is also subject to obliquity, which is the angle the Earth's axis of rotation tilts in relation to the sun, as well as precession, how the Earth wobbles on its axis and affects Earth's rotation. The eccentricity cycle lasts around 100,000 years, while obliquity is 40,000 years and precession is 20,000 years. A study of core sample taken from various places on Earth and a correlation of these with fluctuations in the Earth's orbit seems to suggest that changes in climate may be linked to these orbital changes.

While fluctuations in planetary orbital cycles are generally accepted as at least part of the cause of warming and cooling during the Pleistocene Epoch, the precise mechanism by which these temperature changes occurred is not understood. Orbital fluctuations alone do not seem to be able to account for global temperature changes associated with ice ages. It has also been pointed out that changes due to obliquity should logically cancel each other out – as the planet wobbles in its orbit, that might expose one hemisphere to less sunlight, but that should mean that the other hemisphere gets more. To explain this, it has been suggested that there are additional "feedback" mechanics involved which amplify relatively small temperature changes. For example, the albedo (reflectivity) of the Earth is changed by the accumulation of snow and ice in northern regions. Increased albedo reflects more heat back out into space and leads to lowering temperatures. Core samples also suggest that CO_2 levels were lower during ice ages and may have amplified the relatively minor temperature changes caused by orbital fluctuation as CO_2 helped to trap heat near the planet surface – the greenhouse effect. These feedback mechanisms may have contributed to making the Earth even cooler during cold periods, though we cannot be precisely certain of their cause or relationship.

Since the peak of the last Ice Age around 18 kya, the Earth has been steadily warming. The glaciers that still exist are slowly melting remnants of the last glacial period. However, it is possible that orbital fluctuations may yet see the planet return to a much colder climate. Perhaps one of the most surprising things about the Pleistocene and its many ice ages was that the temperature was not a great deal lower than it is today. Most studies suggest that the global temperature was only on average around four degrees cooler than today. However, that was sufficient to make enormous changes to the surface of the planet.

There were other changes on the planet that were a direct result of these temperature changes. For example, so much of the planet's water was trapped as ice that precipitation virtually stopped for long periods, leading to sharp declines in sea levels. At some periods, the overall sea level may have been as much as four hundred feet lower than its present day level. As temperatures rose, so did sea levels. This was exacerbated by massive deluges of fresh water as glaciers melted and this in turn caused shifts in ocean flows. Added to this, changing temperatures caused sudden changes in atmospheric circulation and the advance and retreat of vegetation belts across all the continents.

The changes between warm and cold periods could happen quite suddenly. It is believed that some of the warm periods developed over a relatively short period, perhaps no more than a few hundred years, in some cases perhaps as little as a decade, though the accumulation of ice and glaciers appears to have taken much longer.

The development of flora and fauna on Earth was dominated by these cycles. Some species became habituated to living in Arctic conditions and thrived as the ice sheets moved south. Other species needed warmer conditions and retreated from the ice sheets to more temperate zones.

Flora and Fauna during the Pleistocene Epoch

The flora of the Pleistocene Epoch was not markedly different from the flora of today. There were some conifers, including pine, spruce, cypress and yew, as well as smaller numbers of broadleaf trees such as beech and oak. On the ground, there were prairie grasses as well as members of the lily, orchid and rose families. Close to the ice sheets, the landscape was generally open with grasses and a few trees, resembling modern northern tundra. Further from the ice, boreal forests of spruce and pine covered much of the landscape.

Perhaps surprisingly, even during the most extensive ice ages, the climate on the parts of the planet not covered by ice was fairly temperate. Summers were cooler than they are now, but only by a matter of a few degrees and winters were actually milder. It seems that the vast northern ice sheets acted as a barrier to the masses of freezing air from the Arctic that bring cold winter weather today. Overall, the climate of the Pleistocene Epoch seems to have been fairly settled and temperate outside the areas directly affected by ice.

The fauna of the Pleistocene Epoch included many large herbivores and carnivores that are now extinct. These large creatures (i.e. with an adult body weight of over 44 kilograms or 97 lbs.), the megafauna, of this period are some of the most fascinating in Earth's recent history. The following is not an exhaustive look at the megafauna of the Pleistocene, but a brief discussion of some of the best-known species from that time.

Mammoth. One of the most instantly recognizable megafauna of the Pleistocene Epoch is the mammoth. The earliest known examples of proboscideans, the clade that includes modern elephants, first appeared around 55 mya. The first of the genus *Mammuthus*, a sub-group of this clade, first appeared in the Pliocene Epoch around 5 mya. The second mammoth, the African mammoth, *Mammuthus africanavus* ("*African ancestor mammoth*") appeared during the early Pleistocene and fossils have been found in north and central Africa. However, like many early mammoths, this example does not accord with the popular image of a mammoth. It was relatively small and lacked the thick coat of hair that characterized many later mammoths. However, *Mammuthus africanavus* is thought by some paleontologists to be the ancestor of all the mammoths that followed.

There were a bewildering number of Mammoth species, almost all of which emerged during the Pleistocene. *Mammuthus trogontherii*, or the steppe mammoth, for example, appeared during the mid-Pleistocene and was a truly enormous creature. It resembled a modern elephant but stood almost four and a half meters (14.7 feet) tall, compared to the 3.2 meters (10.5 feet) of today's African bush elephant. Steppe mammoths, as the name suggests, ranged across the grassy plains of the Pleistocene and principally ate grass. It had teeth specially evolved to grind the vast quantities of grass needed to sustain its massive body weight. Mature male steppe mammoths had very large and elaborately curved tusks, with some examples reaching almost five meters (16.4 feet) in length!

Perhaps the best-known mammoth of all is *Mammuthus primigenius*, more generally known as the wooly mammoth or the tundra mammoth. Not quite as large as the steppe mammoth, this species was wonderfully adapted to survive in very cold conditions. Under its skin, it had a thick layer of fat. On the skin itself, it had two thick layers of hair - an undercoat mainly used to provide insulation, and a longer outer coat (with hair up to one meter in length), which provided protection from rain and snow. Even the woolly mammoth's ears were adapted to cold conditions. Modern elephants have large ears that help to dissipate heat, but the wooly mammoth had very small ears in order to conserve heat. The wooly mammoth had large tusks and it is thought that these may have been used to sweep layers of snow off potential food sources, such as grass and small saplings. Small populations of wooly mammoth actually survived beyond the end of the Pleistocene; it is believed that the last examples may still have been alive less than 2,000 years ago, though this fascinating creature is now wholly extinct.

Vast herds of mammoth ranged across an enormous area during the Pleistocene. What has become known as a *mammoth steppe* stretched all the way from present-day Spain and Portugal, across present-day Europe and Asia and even across the Bering Land Bridge into present-day Alaska and the Yukon.

Mastodon. Closely related to the mammoth is the mastodon, another elephant-like mammal that seems to have existed mainly in what is now North America. These were very large, in many cases larger than present-day elephants, and lacked the long hair of the woolly mammoth. This creature seems to have lived large herds mainly in woodlands in colder areas. Although they looked similar, the mastodon was not related to the mammoth and is characterized by shorter, more powerful legs and musculature.

Sabre-toothed Cats. Another very well-known species from the Pleistocene are the *Homotherium*, ferocious saber-toothed cats. These were large feline predators characterized by prominent, curved canine teeth. There were several species of these large predators during the Pleistocene with some reaching a height of over one meter (3.3 feet) at the shoulder and a weight of over four hundred pounds – comparable with today's adult male African lion. These creatures first emerged during the Pliocene Epoch, around 5 mya.

The most notable feature of these predators, apart from their distinctive teeth, was that all saber-toothed species had front and rear limbs of different length, with the front legs being longer than the rear – meaning these cats' legs would have resembled a modern hyena. It is believed these animals hunted in packs and likely ran-down their prey in the same manner as today's large modern cats, such as the lion.

There were up to fifteen different (though similar) species of these apex predators in the Pleistocene and it seems that they predominated at higher latitudes, most likely feeding on the herds of mammoth and other smaller creatures. The best-known was *Smilodon*, more popularly known as the saber-toothed tiger, though it is was not related to the modern tiger or any other modern big cat. Smilodon remains have mainly been found in North America where they likely hunted bison and camels. The last of the *Homotherium* are thought to have become extinct around 30,000 years ago.

Bear. Several species of bear existed during the Pleistocene, and some of these reached a truly terrifying size. *Arctodus*, for example, more commonly known as the short-faced bear, stood up to 3.5 meters (11.5 feet) tall and weighed up to 800 kg (1,700 lbs.). That makes it notably larger than the biggest modern bear, the Grizzly (*Ursus arctos horriblis*). While its size clearly made the short-faced bear formidable, modern research suggests it was likely a scavenger rather than an apex predator, possibly obtaining up to thirty percent of its food from plants and berries. Another formidable Pleistocene bear was the cave bear (*Ursus spelaeus*), so called because many remains of this creature have been discovered in caves, leading to speculation that it likely lived in caves rather than using them only for napping or hibernating. Only slightly smaller than the short-faced bear, the cave bear stood up to 11 feet tall and weighed up to 600kg (1,322 lbs.). In 2020, reindeer hunters in Russia made an astonishing discovery on Bolshoy Lyakhovsky Island in the Lyakhovsky Islands archipelago in the seas off eastern Russia: the preserved carcass of a cave bear. All the soft tissue was still intact, including the nose – something that generally decays quickly. Soon after, the preserved carcass of a cave bear cub was discovered in the same location. It is estimated they most likely died between 20,000-40,000 years ago, but their carcasses provide a good picture of what this fearsome creature looked like when alive.

The cave bear seems to have lived mainly in areas of low mountains, avoiding the steppes and open country. One notable factor is that some caves have revealed thousands of cave bear bones, leading to speculation that these animals may have lived and hunted in large herds, a truly frightening notion.

Dire Wolves. Another well-known carnivore from the Pleistocene was *Canis dirus* (fearsome dog), better known as the dire wolf. This was one of the largest wolves to have existed, larger than the largest wolves found today. A study of dire wolf skulls suggests that it also had a particularly powerful bite, much more powerful than modern wolves or dingoes. This suggests the dire wolf adapted to attack large prey, perhaps even attacking mammoths. Like most wolves, the dire wolf is thought to have hunted as part of a pack. Most dire wolf remains have been found in North America, though the Pleistocene saw many other varieties of wolf including the Pleistocene gray wolf (larger than the modern wolf) and other canine predators such as the Pleistocene coyote (*Canis latrans*).

Of course, not all large Pleistocene mammals were apex predators. The **wooly rhinoceros** (*Coelodonta antiquitatis*), for example, was a massive herbivore, similar to the modern rhinoceros, but like the wooly mammoth, it was covered in a thick layer of hair to allow it to survive in cold environments. *Megaloceros,* the **giant elk**, was a very large ancestor of today's fallow deer; large herds of these herbivores roamed the woodlands and meadows of the Pleistocene.

Many of the creatures of the Pleistocene were very large compared to their counterparts today, and that applied not only to those on the land, but also those in the skies. *Teratornithidae* was a family of very large birds of prey that included several species. **Teratornis incredibilis** is one of the largest known birds capable of flight, with a wingspan of up to 5.5 meters (16 feet) and weighing up to 23kg (50 lbs.). Comparing that to the largest flying bird today, the wandering albatross, that has a wingspan of up to 3.3 meters (11 feet), gives some idea of just how large and powerful these birds must have been. A few remains have been found of what may have been an even larger teratorn, **Argentavis magnificens**, a Condor-like bird that may have had a wingspan of up to 6.4 meters (21 feet).

The one thing that links these Pleistocene animals with others is that all had become extinct by the end of the Pleistocene Epoch, including **Castoroides,** a giant beaver as large as some present-day bears; the **Glyptodon**, a giant relative of the present-day armadillo; and **Megatherium**, the giant ground sloth. The precise reasons for this sudden mass extinction of species is a matter of debate and disagreement that will be discussed further below.

The Emergence of Humans
All life can be traced back to single-celled life forms approximately 4 billion years ago. It was not until the early Paleozoic Era around 500 mya that the first vertebrates begin appearing in the fossil record. It is very possible that these types of life forms date back even earlier but either were not preserved in the fossil record or have yet to be uncovered by scientists.

In the Paleozoic Era, there were several varieties of fish, amphibians, and reptiles. By the end of this geological period, around 250 mya, mammal-like reptiles begin to appear that may be the earliest ancestors of mammals. During this period in Earth's history, the position of the continents was vastly different from what it is today, and through continental drift, the crusts of the earth were shifting and colliding resulting in volcanic activity and earthquakes. During the Paleozoic and earlier, the continents are believed to have formed a single supercontinent known as Pangea. The landmasses began drifting apart, and it was not until around 65 mya that the positions of the landmasses shifted to roughly where they are today.

A map depicting Pangea

These environmental factors had a significant influence on the evolution of life. Land animals such as primates became isolated from one another, and following an early extinction level event came the Mesozoic Era, which took place from around 225 mya until another extinction level event 65 mya. During this time, dinosaurs dominated the landscape, the air, and the sea, but the earliest definite mammals also began to enter the fossil record. Meanwhile, the earliest example of placental mammals dates to 70 mya, or near the end of the Mesozoic Era.

This form of mammalian evolutionary adaptation continued into the Cenozoic Era and until the present day, and it is found in a majority of mammal species. The Cenozoic Era is divided into seven distinct epochs: the Paleocene, Eocene, Oligocene, Miocene, Pliocene, Pleistocene, and Holocene, which is the present period.

When the Mesozoic Era ended with an extinction level event that wiped out a majority of life forms such as the dinosaurs and others, this allowed the ecological resources that were previously dominated by these animals to suddenly be available to the survivors. One type of animal that survived this event was a small mammal that would have been about the size of a rodent, and these mammals quickly became successful species within the newly opened up environment (Dawkins 2005).

One physical adaptation that allowed them to be more successful than the reptiles involved the size of the brain. In order for mammals to process more information relating to learning, the brain needs to be larger. During this period, there was an increase in the size of the brain. In particular, there was a size increase in the cerebrum and the neocortex (which deals with higher brain function). The brain also began to develop more wrinkles or convolutions, which allowed more surface area and thereby allowed for more neurons (nerve cells). This development of the brain is linked with the long period of growth that takes place internally during pregnancy (Dawkins 2009, 209–250). Reptiles, birds, and most kinds of fish externally deposit their young and allow them to incubate for a time.

Placental mammals (as opposed to monotreme mammals that lay eggs or marsupials which have pouches for their offspring) with a longer in utero period allow for more intense growth to occur, which is then continued in childhood. After birth, the period during which the offspring is reliant upon the mother for milk allows for more complex neural structures to form. It is also during this close interaction period that social interactions and learning opportunities have an impact on the development of the brain. This influence of constant learning at such a young age, which comes about through observation and interaction, has a profound effect on the development of the brain.

Mammals also had a variety of dentition that allowed them to more easily adapt to environmental resources. In contrast to certain reptiles such as the alligator, which only has a single type of specialized tooth, mammal dentition was made up of teeth for cutting (incisors), biting (canines), and smashing or grinding (premolars and molars).

The ability of mammals to maintain a consistent internal body temperature through endothermic processes also likely contributed to their success relative to other non-mammals. This separated the mammals and birds, or certain descendants of dinosaurs, from reptiles that rely on the environment to raise their body temperature (Jurmain et al 2004). By not relying as much on exposure to sunlight, the mammals were better able to disperse and expand the resources available to them. In essence, they could venture to more northern or southern latitudes where exposure to the sun was not as intense.

The fossil evidence of early primate life forms during the Paleocene is difficult to interpret because it consists mainly of fragments of jaws and teeth. The interpretations of this evidence are often debated among paleontologists, specifically regarding whether certain forms belong to the primate order or not. More complete evidence is found in the Eocene (55–34 mya), during which over 200 species have been recognized (Dawkins 2009, 143–180). It is from this array of primate species that scientists can say with more certainty that these are primates that were widely distributed (across North America, Europe, and Asia, which were connected at the time) and went extinct at the end of the Eocene. However, it is still debated to what extent these species are directly related to living primates.

During the end of the Eocene and the beginning of the Oligocene (34–23 mya), the first evidence of anthropoids (a suborder of primates that include monkeys, apes and humans) begins to appear in the fossil record. The majority of fossils come from Egypt at the Fayum site. During this time, continental drift would have separated Old and New World anthropoid species, thereby creating a founder effect in either the Old or New World evolution of certain anthropoids. Other possibilities are that early primitive monkeys "rafted" to the New World through some sort of large storm in a manner similar to the way the Galapagos Islands were populated by non-swimming tortoises.

It would not be until the Miocene (23–5 mya) that early hominids began to appear. Across Asia, Africa, and Europe a new type of hominid began to emerge, and new evolutionary developments were taking place. Given the wide geographic distribution of the hominoids, there was not a single species of hominoid but many more than there are today (a group of apes and humans). As such, there were a number of evolutionary developments thanks to the changes in geography, climate and resources available, and climate in particular was a major issue that was affecting all hominoids during the Miocene.

The continents were roughly in the position that they can be found today. The impact of the South Asian tectonic plate into Asia had created the Himalayas and South America, and Australia had drifted further away from Antartica. These shifts made the climate of the Miocene dramatically warmer than the Oligocene period. The drifting Arabian plate also settled into northeastern Africa, allowing populations of hominids to travel more easily into Asia, which occurred around 16 mya.

Dated fossils show that hominids were active in Africa approximately 23-14 mya, while they were active in Europe 13–11 mya and in Asia 16-7 mya. Although there is an abundance of fossils from this period, they are still poorly understood in the context of human evolution. What can be said with a reasonable degree of certainty is that these hominids are more closely related to modern apes and humans than they are to Old World monkeys, and that they had larger bodies that more closely resemble orangutans, gorillas, chimpanzees, and humans than other small apes, such as gibbons. A definite lineage that led to hominids has not yet been discovered, although it is during the late Miocene that hominid fossils begin to appear.

The emergence of hominids during the late Miocene can be identified in the fossils due to the evolutionary changes that took place in the hominid population. As mentioned earlier, which hominoid species are directly related to the late hominid lineage is not understood, but the evolutionary changes and an understanding of the changing environment during this period offer clues as to what influenced these evolutionary adaptations in hominids. These adaptations did not all take place at the same time, developing over millions of years and at various rates.

The most obvious feature and distinguishing characteristic of hominids is the ability to walk on two legs. Referred to as being bipedal, the ability walk upright is a characteristic that can be found in modern non-human apes as well. For short distances and with a bit of a struggle, non-human apes can walk for short distances, sometimes even while carrying other objects, but the distance covered is typically short and ineffective. The hominids, on the other hand, mastered the ability to walk on two legs for greater distances and with little difficulty (meaning the efficiency in walking burned fewer calories in the process). In order to walk effectively, the body needs to be erect, and this is a characteristic that can be seen today in modern primates through social activities such as grooming, feeding and even sleeping.

It is likely that the early ancestors of humans acted in a similar manner. These early ancestors also likely spent a significant amount of time in the trees, but some sort of event, or motivator, eventually brought the early ancestors of man to the ground, which further encouraged the ability to be bipedal. Although the exact factor is unknown, one theory is that the change in climate began to reduce the amount of forest or jungle available. In place of these jungles in Africa, there may have been more open grassland similar to that which can be found today.

There are numerous benefits to being able to walk on two legs when exposed and out in the open. Standing on two legs may have initially developed as a mode of looking out for predators while not in the jungle, as the ability to stand on two legs allowed greater distance to be seen, especially if standing on two legs allowed one to see over tall grasses. Thus, the hominids may have started out walking on all fours, pausing to stand and look out, then continuing to walk on all fours. The benefit of being able to walk for longer periods while looking out for predators may have allowed these individuals to survive and reproduce more than those who could only pause to stand and look for predators. This type of posturing can still be found in modern baboons that frequent the savannas of Africa.

Another physical benefit that would have favored upright posture and walking involves the climate. The African savanna receives a tremendous amount of sun, which then radiates heat from the ground. At certain times of the day, such as at noon, the angle of the sun rays to the ground is around 90 degrees. Quadrupeds expose more of their body to direct sunlight when out in the open, which causes their bodies to easily overheat. Bipedal animals, on the other hand, expose far less of their bodies directly to the sunlight, thereby keeping their bodies cooler during the day. Quadrupeds are also lower to the ground while it is radiating heat from the sunlight, causing additional warming of the body, whereas bipedal animals keep their bodies farther from the ground.

Being bipedal also frees the forelimbs, or arms, allowing them to carry resources, whether it was food or material for shelter. This benefit may have allowed individuals to venture further or more successfully from the jungle and also return with resources not available in the jungle. Eventually, after a few million years of adapting to life on the ground, the ability to use one's hands for the manipulation of material would become useful in the production of tools. This would have encouraged bio-cultural evolution, a process in which individuals are favored within the population based on the culture that was present.

The ability to make tools would also further encourage the ability to be bipedal as hominids transitioned from scavenging carrion from the savanna to hunting big game. By burning less calories and keeping the body cooler during the day, bipedal hominids could become more effective big game hunters.

Modern day hunter-gatherers employ a hunting tactic that is likely similar to how hunting was carried out by early human ancestors. A small band of hunters will pursue a large animal such as a giraffe during a hot period of the day. The large animal will quickly flee the hunters, causing the animal to overheat and tire. The hunters will pursue at a casual pace, tracking the animal. Bipedalism is effective at covering long distances, whereas the quadruped animal is better suited for evading fast predators over a short distance. After chasing down the giraffe time and again, never giving it a chance to fully recover, the animal is eventually exhausted and can be killed more easily by the hunters. Such large game provides a significant amount of calories to the hunters, who may consume some of the animal there and carry what's left back to the families.

Modern apes, such as chimpanzees, can only ineffectively walk because their hind limbs are more suited for grasping (Gribbon and Cherfas 2001), but over time hominids lost the use to effectively grasp branches with their feet. Functionally, each foot needs to be able to accept the entire weight of the body and balance while the other foot lands on the heel and catches the weight of the body while walking. The center of gravity during this locomotion must also be balanced, and to do so, the knees of the hominid come narrowly together while walking. The leg also evolved to allow full extension of the knee while the pelvis became more "bowl" shaped.

Conversely, the chimpanzee's bone structure is more ideal for the trunk of the animal to be parallel with the ground, and the rib cage in this posture essentially holds the internal organs in the right place. The rib cage of a bipedal hominid with an upright trunk has the internal organs being pulled downwards by gravity. Being bipedal thus necessitated changes to the pelvis that allowed it to support the internal organs in a comfortable manner.

Another structural change that facilitated being bipedal was the location of the foramen magnum, the hole that assists in the support of the head. In quadrupeds, the foramen is located more towards the back of the skull so that the animal may look forwards, but in bipeds, the foramen is located more underneath the skull so that the biped may look forward while standing.

The spine also developed two curves that assist in keeping the center of weight above the pelvis. Eventually, the lower limbs of humans elongated allowing for greater movement (White 2011).

While there is wide agreement on the defining characteristics of hominids and the evolutionary patterns, the dating and classifications that are being used are constantly changing as new discoveries are being made and new dating techniques develop. In the short period of a decade, one textbook changed the "earliest" hominid date from 3-7 mya (Jurmain et al 2004: 191).

One of the earliest species of the genus Homo to be discovered is *Homo habilis*, which basically means "handy man." The name comes from the belief at the time of its discovery that this species was the first to start using stone tools. The first fossils to be uncovered in Olduvai Gorge were from the same stratigraphic layer as simple stone tools. Fossils of the crania and postcranial skeleton for this species have been found in both eastern and southern Africa and date to around 2.5–1.6 mya.

Cicero Moraes' picture of a facial reconstruction of *Homo habilis*

The remains of a skull

Given the gradual changes that take place in evolution, *Homo habilis* shares a number of characteristics that are similar to the genus Australopithecus, such as in the postcranial elements. That said, the size and shape of the *Homo habilis* skull are markedly different.

The size of the brain is much larger relative to the size of the body, being around 680 cc. In order to house a larger brain, the skull features a more vertical frontal bone, creating a more vertical forehead. The brow ridges that sit on the lower portion of the frontal bone are also reduced in size. Other reductions in the face include reduced prognathism and a reduction in the size of the premolars and molars.

Postcranial elements display clear signs of bipedalism, such as the large toe being in line with the other toes instead being off to the side as they are in modern apes. Furthermore, the arches of the foot are present, allowing the full weight of the body to be supported and act as a shock absorber when walking. The leg bones are also longer than in Australopithecus, but *Homo habilis* retained long arms. Other primitive features include hand and finger bones that would have made climbing in the trees easier. The robustness of the finger bones is more comparable to those of modern apes than humans. There is also an attachment site present for a leg muscle that is particularly useful in climbing, suggesting that there was still some amount of time spent climbing.

There is a wide variation of traits found in this species, and given the fragmentary nature of some of the elements, it is possible that they belong to other species of Homo like *Homo rudolfensis*. Another possibility is that sexual dimorphism was more pronounced in *Homo habilis* than previously thought.

What is generally accepted is that *Homo habilis* was capable of making stone tools. These tools were flakes that were broken off from a core and had sharp edges. These tools could serve a number of purposes, such as cutting up the remains of an animal or cleaning its skin. But while *Homo habilis* almost certainly used tools, scholars still debate which species of Homo actually began making stone tools first since the species *Homo rudolfensis* also lived during the same time.

During this period in Africa, the environment was undergoing a major shift in climate, and the closed forests with readily available lakes and streams were being replaced by more open savanna and arid conditions. It is possible that these environmental changes, which began around 2.5 mya, spurred the development of the genus Homo. Around 2 mya, the climate began shifting back towards being warm and humid, and based on other associated faunal fossils, *Homo habilis* likely lived in forested areas with access to streams and lakes.

Living at the same time as *Homo habilis* was *Homo rudolfensis*, with a slightly earlier date of 2.1–1.8 mya. Just like *Homo habilis*, *Homo rudolfensis* were in eastern and southern Africa and displayed morphological characteristics that are similar to the early ancestors of the Australopithecus genus.

Homo rudolfensis had a cranial capacity of around 750 cc (larger than its *Homo habilis* contemporary). Despite this larger brain, the face was much broader, containing larger molars and premolars and larger orbits for the eyes. The inclusion of such large molars and premolars, a trait characteristic of Australopithecus species, has led some to argue that *Homo rudolfensis* belongs with this genus instead.

The mix of primitive and derived traits makes the understanding of this species within human evolution difficult. Moreover, classifying fossils between *Homo habilis* and *Homo rudolfensis* has been difficult and has led to more confusion surrounding these species. It is possible that these two species are actually one species, and the differences are only the result of sexual dimorphism. This is rather difficult to demonstrate, however, since the only recovered fossil remains of *Homo rudolfensis* are from the crania. In other words, there are no limb or trunk bones with which to compare the full body sizes of *Homo rudolfensis* and *Homo habilis*.

That said, the tooth wear pattern of *Homo rudolfensis* suggests that the diet of this species differed from *Homo habilis*. The grinding pattern of the larger molars and premolars of *Homo rudolfensis* indicates that a significant amount of grinding was being done. It is likely that *Homo rudolfensis* was capable of consuming tough fruits and plants that required a large amount of chewing. This is in contrast to *Homo habilis* tooth wear, which indicate *Homo habilis* had a diet of meat and plants.

The debate over which Homo species is the direct ancestor of modern humans is important for understanding the evolutionary developments of these other branching species. In this instance, the development of a larger brain must have occurred independently if *Homo habilis* was the direct ancestor. On the other hand, if *Homo rudolfensis* was a direct ancestor, then the large primitive features of the face may have also developed independently from earlier ancestors.

Around 1.8 mya, a third species of Homo appeared in the fossil record. *Homo erectus* would have shared the landscape for a time with *Homo habilis* and *Homo rudolfensis*, but the fossils of *Homo erectus* are not limited to eastern and southern Africa. Instead, they are found across Africa and parts of mainland and insular Asia. This is the first species of Homo to be found outside Africa (Rightmire 1993).

Features of *Homo erectus* suggest an evolution toward modern humans, and the features which separate *Homo erectus* from the other Homo species are found in the skull. The size of the brain was approximately 900 cc, making it larger than the brain size of *Homo habilis*. *Homo erectus* would not have the largest brain capacity of the Homo genus during its existence, with the emergence of *Homo heidelbergensis* approximately 800,000 years ago. The larger brain size may not matter much when the size of the brain is considered with the size of the body, which also increased.

The development of the skull also changed in *Homo erectus*. While the body became larger, the brain case did not become more vertical relative to the body, resulting in a sloping and long appearance similar to an American football. Other features that developed on the skull are thicker brow ridges and the development of bony projections at the rear of the skull (Gilbert and Asfaw 2008).

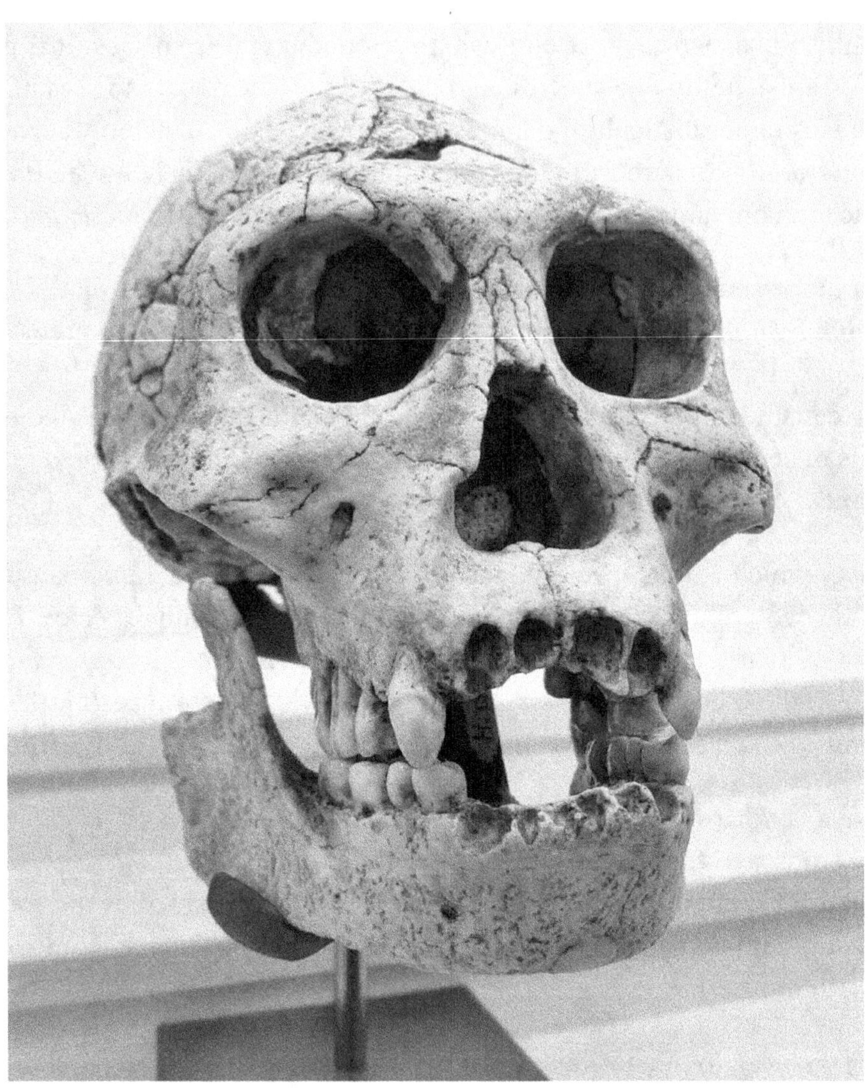

The skull of a *Homo erectus*

While the facial features of *Homo erectus* would have made them noticeably different if they were alive today, their postcranial morphology may have been similar to modern humans. A key difference is the density or thickness of the bones; in *Homo erectus* the limb bones are more robust, but otherwise they appear very similar to modern humans. The length of the hindlimbs in relation to the arms is similar to modern humans, which means that *Homo erectus* may have been able to walk in a similar way. (Richtmire 1993: 57–84). This may or may not be linked with the widespread distribution of *Homo erectus*.

Perhaps more important for *Homo erectus* than simply being able to walk out of Africa would have been the ability to adapt to changing climates and essentially modify the environment around them. Most notably, the major advantage that *Homo erectus* would have had is the ability to control fire. This skill, which no other animal has mastered, helped *Homo erectus* travel across the world, and it may date as far back as 1.7 mya to as recently as 200,000 years ago. Most scientists agree that *Homo erectus* was able to control fire by at least 600,000 years ago, and anatomically modern humans were able to create and use fire 150,000 years ago. The early species of Homo would have been familiar with the effects of fire, from the devastation it could cause to jungle habitats to the rapid spreading wildfires of the savanna. These fires would have killed and burned animals that early Homo would have found while scavenging after a natural fire.

Once the benefit of fire was understood, early Homo could begin to control fire by taking it where it was needed. Following a natural fire, *Homo erectus*, or perhaps another species of Homo, likely would have attempted to harness the power of fire by bringing it to another location, such as a camp. Since this was the only means of possessing fire until the ability to start one was discovered, the fire would have been kept ablaze for as long as possible. The first benefit of fire that would have been easily recognizable would be the warmth it provided. This, along with the invention of clothing via animal skins, would be the beginning of mankind's manipulation of the environment for survival. Not only would *Homo erectus* be able to stay warm through the night, they could survive in otherwise deadly freezing temperatures. The fear that other animals had of fire would be another benefit that *Homo erectus* would use to its advantage in its conquest over the animal kingdom, as fire would provide protection from nocturnal predators that would have preyed upon the vulnerable species.

Some of the earliest archaeological evidence for the use of fire is found in caves since the sheltered area is not regularly eroded with water and weather, which also make caves ideal for animals to live in. Before the harnessing of fire, *Homo erectus* would have had to share or fight for control of these caves at great risk, but the fear that animals had of fire helped *Homo erectus* clear these shelters of any potential threats and keep them out.

This tactic could also be applied to hunting animals. Recognizing that animals would flee in a certain direction from fire, *Homo erectus* could start grassfires to direct the animals into a corral, off a cliff, or into killing zones where the animals would be slaughtered and cooked. This method of hunting would have provided an abundance of food that would have been hard to come by before. Typically, early Homo would have scavenged for meat from the carcasses left behind by larger hunters, but with fire, mankind could obtain the prime parts of the animal and cook them (Wrangham 2010, 101).

Early man also would have noticed the changes fire made to meat while scavenging for food after a forest or bush fire. Most notably, cooked meat was easier to chew and easier to digest. Eating raw uncooked food would cost 15–35% more energy, or calories, than eating cooked food, and saving these valuable extra calories allowed for evolutionary changes to develop. Changes can be seen in *Homo erectus* that may reflect the use of fire and the benefits of cooking. The teeth for example, were reduced in size, which indicates a softer diet that did not require as much tearing and grinding as before. Furthermore, the brain was becoming larger, suggesting a diet of higher quality foods.

Another advantage to the cooking of food, though they couldn't have known it at the time, was that the heat killed dangerous parasites and pathogens in the food, thereby potentially extending the lifespan of those who ate the cooked food. The improved survival rate allowed *Homo erectus* to increase in number and meant that new generations could also learn the benefits of fire for modifying tools.

The ability of *Homo erectus* and later Homo species to harness fire also allowed them to increase the effectiveness of their tools, providing a large technological advancement. Fire could be used to harden wooden spears, which allowed Homo species to hunt a variety of animals more successfully. One archaeological site in Germany associated with *Homo heidelbergensis* (discussed further below) contained eight fire-hardened wood spears that were used to hunt horses (Coolidge and Wynn 2009, 151–179). Another site in Germany also featured fire-hardened spears that were used for hunting "straight-tusked elephants". The tactics for these hunts changed from using the spears for throwing, as would be the case for non-hardened spears, to thrusting the spears.

The hardening effect of fire was also used to create ritual objects. While figures from the same time were carved from stone or bone, other figures were created from clay that were then fired like pottery. All of this evidence suggests that many important interactions from all parts of life took place around fires, and these close interactions around the fire would have assisted in the development of culture and communication between individuals, eventually spurring on the development of language and societies. Put short, fire became the most important tool in mankind's evolution.

Once a group of *Homo erectus* had drifted far enough away from another group of *Homo erectus*, the geographical separation, combined with the unique pressures of environmental factors and natural selection, would eventually lead to the formation of a new species. The portion of *Homo erectus* that stayed in Africa would begin to follow a different evolutionary path than those who moved to Europe and Asia.

There are two general theories regarding the spread of *Homo erectus* out of Africa. The first one is that around 1.5 mya, *Homo erectus* migrated from Africa in various waves, perhaps by hunting migrating herds. This theory posits that *Homo erectus* migrated to separate regions and eventually developed independent from those who became *Homo sapiens*. This theory would then place the Neanderthals as an intermediate phase between *Homo erectus* and *Homo sapiens*. Another hypothesis is that *Homo erectus* left Africa roughly 1.5 mya and continued to evolve outside of Africa, but it was only in Africa that *Homo sapiens* developed and left Africa in a "second" wave around 150,000 years ago into Europe and Asia. This second wave of early *Homo sapiens* then encountered Neanderthals in Europe and Asia and eventually replaced their evolutionary cousins (Steadman 2009: 69). This second theory is the one most subscribed to by anthropologists and supported by fossil and genetic evidence.

Fossils of early Neanderthals before 130,000 years ago are rare, but after this point they become much more common in European and Asian sites, and the name Neanderthal is based on the discovery of what quarry workers believed were bear fossils from the Neander Valley near Düsseldorf in Germany. In 1856, workers from a limestone quarry brought the fossilized remains to a local natural science teacher, Johann Carl Fuhlrott, who recognized the fragmented remains as one of the "most ancient races of man" (Leakey 1981: 146). His assumption was based on the low, prominent brow ridges and stout limb bones. This finding was confirmed by anatomy expert Hermann Schaaffhausen, who also believed these bones to belong to a "race" that was a few thousand years old.

Fuhlrott

Schaaffhausen

Meanwhile, the rest of the academic world was not so convinced that the Neanderthals were part of the human race, or at least not a "normal" ancestor. German scientists in particular were convinced that the stout bowed legs indicated that the person was a horse rider for most of their life. This observation just happened to fit the recent history of the area - in 1814, Russian cavalry had crossed the landscape chasing Napoleon's French soldiers near the end of the Napoleonic Wars. Other theories posited were that the bowed legs were the result of rickets, an osteopathology that developed from a vitamin deficiency and caused enough pain to make the person habitually furrow their brow, resulting in a thicker bone structure above the eyes (Leakey 1981: 146).

As time went on, more fossils with similar characteristics forced the scientific community to accept the Neanderthals as a genuine hominid lineage (Jurmain et al 2004: 256). Other specimens were turning up in European countires outside of Germany, and in southwestern France in 1908, the specimen examined by Boule was uncovered. Even more interestingly, it was reported that the nearly complete skeleton was uncovered in a burial. The body had been deposited in a fetal position with fragments of non-human bone placed over the body. Surrounding the body in the burial were flint tools and more fragments of non-human bones. Despite these findings, Boule still considered both the individual and the Neanderthals in general to belong to a brutish savage race.

Another site in France, the Moula-Guercy cave, produced around 78 broken hominid fragments associated with the Neanderthals. These remains, uncovered in the late 21st century, have been dated to between 100,000–120,000 years ago. A more recent Neanderthal site in St. Césaire, France, had fossils that date to approximately 35,000 years ago. This site contained worked animal remains and a variety of tools commonly associated with the Neanderthals. Another cave site in Zafarraya, Spain has also produced fossils from relatively recent Neanderthals. In this site, the remains have been dated to as recently as 29,000 years ago (Jurmain et al 2004: 257–258). Recent dating of another cave site in central Europe also places the Neanderthals as still being alive less than 30,000 years ago. What these sites indicate is that the Neanderthals were sharing the same geographical region as anatomically modern humans for thousands of years, and they may have even been sharing tool production methods.

Neanderthal fossils have also been discovered outside of Europe. In Israel, fossils have been uncovered that share many similarities to those of the European Neanderthals but are noticeably less robust. Perhaps the most famous of these finds comes from Mugharet-et-Tabun, or Cave of the Oven, in Israel. The site was first excavated in the 1930s, but modern scientific tests indicate the finds were about 120,000 years old. Like the finds in Europe, this would make the Neanderthals a contemporary of modern humans, whose fossils have also been discovered in caves in the surrounding areas.

Another important find from the area comes from Kebara. In this cave system, a hyoid bone (the floating bone located in the throat) was discovered that dates to about 60,000 years old. This bone is believed to belong to a Neanderthal since it was found with a nearly complete Neanderthal pelvis. Scientists were able to use this discovery in order to help learn about Neanderthal culture, especially their language skills.

Another site that has provided an interesting insight into the Neanderthals was found in the Zagros Mountains of Iraq. Here, an individual, known as Shandir 1, was uncovered and dated to about 60,000 years ago. This person had suffered from a considerable amount of physical trauma, yet they had managed to live to the age of 30-45. In order for this individual to have survived so long, it is believed that they must have had the help of other people, which would be an indication of culture and social interaction among the Neanderthals (Trinkaus and Shipman 1992: 341).

The Last Glacial Period

As recently as 100,000 years ago, there were a number of different species of humans. Most of these stayed in a particular habitat, mainly woodlands, though they spread to these habitats in a number of areas. *Homo sapiens* seem to have been the only species sufficiently adaptable to live in virtually any environment on Earth. This was not because *Home sapiens* was particularly good at any one thing, but rather because they were simply more adaptable and capable of learning and sharing the new skills required to survive. This has led to the creation of the new term *generalist specialist* to describe the niche that *Homo sapiens* filled. In terms of survival, it seems to be better to be capable of adapting to changing circumstances and environments than to be very good at a fixed set of skills.

This became especially relevant around 80,000 years ago, at the beginning of the Last Glacial Period (LGP), which lasted until around 12,000 years ago. This event is sometimes called the Ice Age, though this is technically incorrect since an Ice Age is a longer period of sustained cold that is characterized by the presence of year-round ice sheets in some areas. The LGP saw several cycles of glacier advance and retreat, but it generally involved lower temperatures and changes in environments. When the LGP began, there were a number of human species. However, by the time it ended, only *Homo sapiens* survived. By being better at adapting to changes, modern humans proved to be more capable of surviving on decreasing food supplies and in a variety of environments.

Over the last 40 million years, the climate on Earth has been gradually cooling; the first ice at the poles did not begin to form until around 35 mya. However, this decline in temperature is not uniform and during its long history, Earth has experienced a number of dramatic fluctuations in surface temperature, some of which led to ice ages. It is believed there have been at least five major ice ages when ice sheets covered much of the world's surface: the Huronian, Cryogenian, Andean-Saharan, late Paleozoic, and the Quaternary – the most recent ice age. The Quaternary began around 2.58 mya and continues to the present day.

During the early part of the Quaternary, the period of fluctuation between glacial and interglacial periods was around 40,000 years, but later this slowed to around 100,000 years with interglacial periods of ten to forty thousand years. It is believed there have been eight ice ages during the last three-quarters of a million years. Although it is often referred to as an ice age, the LGP is simply the most recent glacial period and currently we are simply in an extended interglacial period.

Even within the LGP there was not a steady decrease in temperature or a steady increase in ice sheets. Instead, the climate on Earth underwent a number of dramatic oscillations between warmer and cooler periods. During cooler periods (glacial periods), ice sheets expanded and massive glaciers formed. During warmer periods, when the climate wasn't too different to today (interglacial periods), the ice sheets receded. Our knowledge of the climate during this time comes from a number of sources, but one of the most important is the study of ice cores taken from glaciers in Greenland. Each layer of ice within these cores provides a snapshot of the climate on the planet, and it is through these that scientists have been able to assemble a detailed picture of the changing temperature during the late Pleistocene.

Analysis of Greenland glacier cores revealed at least twenty-five climate cycles, known as Dansgaard-Oeschger, or D-O, cycles. One of the most notable features of these cycles is that warming seems to have happened relatively abruptly, sometimes over the course of a few decades, while cooling took much longer. There is no agreement about what caused these changes. The two most common theories are that these were caused by changes in ocean circulation due to natural changes in the salinity of the North Atlantic (the salt oscillator hypothesis) or by changes in atmospheric circulation (the wind field oscillation hypothesis). However, fairly recently another theory has emerged: erosion from the falling sea levels caused large quantities of dust to enter the atmosphere which contributed to global cooling. Whatever the cause, these changes were dramatic and affected every species on the planet.

By the peak of the LGP, around 20,000 years ago, the average temperature on Earth was ten degrees cooler than today, though in some places it was up to forty degrees cooler. Ice sheets more than two miles thick covered vast areas of the planet including parts of present-day Canada, Scandinavia, Russia and South America. As the temperature dropped, the ice sheets grew and merged until large areas of present-day Europe, Russia and North America were completely covered. Glaciers ground out new valleys as they slowly expanded and sea levels were up to four hundred feet lower than today. Vegetation gradually retreated before the advancing ice and the landscape changed as the temperature rose and fell. For example, in what is today the hot and humid Gulf-coast area of the United States, pine forests and grass prairies were common 20,000 years ago – things that are today found only in the northern US states and Canada.

However, even in glacial periods, the situation was not stable or fixed. Geologists have identified *climate ripples* – bipolar differences in temperature, meaning in general, when it is colder in the north, it is warmer in the south and vice versa. There is no agreement on what causes these ripples. The last climate ripple ended around 12,000 years ago, but just why is a question that has perplexed many generations of scientists.

Scientists can be certain that the changes in climate in the Late Pleistocene were not due to humans; there simply weren't enough of them to have an impact on the global climate. There have been a number of proposed theories for what caused these climate changes and brought about the end of the LGP, though none have yet been universally accepted. It seems likely that the end of the LGP was caused not by a single factor, but by a complex and interrelated set of events that acted together to produce an overall warming that began between eleven and twelve thousand years ago and continues to the present day.

The various factors that affected Earth's climate include the volume of dust trapped in the atmosphere, changes in the circulation of winds and ocean currents, changes in the Earth's orbital attitude and changes in the planet's albedo – increased ice sheets tend to reflect heat back, contributing further to cooling.

There also appears to be a close relationship between CO_2 levels and temperature, though the CO_2 does not itself directly cause the rise in temperature but is rather a kind of feedback mechanism that amplifies its effect. For example, when sea levels drop due to increased glaciation, more land is available for the growth of vegetation. This vegetation absorbs CO_2, causing levels to drop further and causing further cooling. Expanding sea-ice sheets also cover parts of the ocean that might otherwise release CO2 into the atmosphere from deep ocean upwelling.

Since the 1980s, investigation into what caused ice ages and in particular what caused the end of the LGP have intensified. In part, this is due to concerns that climate change is now being driven by human activities – it now seems possible that the human race itself may be adding greenhouse gases to the atmosphere on such a scale that it is actually causing global changes. For this reason, an understanding of the mechanism that caused the LGP to end and for the planet to enter a long period of stable warming is important.

The Late Pleistocene Mass Extinction Event

Towards the end of the Pleistocene Epoch, there were a series of extinctions particularly affecting large animals over 40 kilograms in weight, but these extinctions were not uniform in the precise time that they occurred or in their geographical spread. For example, in Australia somewhere between 40,000 and 24,000 years ago (precise dates have proved difficult to ascertain), there was a mass extinction of large animals and birds that killed around 90% of all species. Before that extinction, Australia was dominated by large marsupials such as giant wombats and kangaroos, as well as by some very large flightless birds. However, as recently as 24,000 years ago, these creatures had all disappeared along with many other species such as long lizards, giant tortoises, and the marsupial lion.

In North America, the late Pleistocene extinction was even more dramatic. Up to 13,000 years ago, North America was the home to large numbers of saber-toothed cats, giant sloths, short-faced bears, giant beavers, mammoths, giant condors, mastodons, lions, dire wolves and a number of large species of pronghorns and llamas. Then around 12,700 years ago, ninety percent of creatures with a weight of over 40kg (99.2 lbs.) in North America became extinct.

This same pattern occurred in other parts of the world as well. In South America, saber-toothed cats, short-faced bears, giant sloths, giant armadillos and many other large species disappeared at the same time.

In Europe and Asia, woolly mammoths, steppe mammoths, saber-toothed cats, dire wolves, short-faced bears, aurochs and several species of rhinoceros all became extinct between 13,000 and 12,000 years ago.

At around the same time in Africa, several species of elephant, lion, tiger and rhinoceros vanished along with aurochs and giant buffalo, giant tapirs, giant lemurs, giant rats and many others.

This was a dramatic extinction not only because it had global reach, but also because it mainly seems to have affected large creatures. It is now generally known as the Late Pleistocene

Megafauna Extinction Event and in areas such as North and South America, there was a loss of all creatures with a body weight over 100kg (220 lbs.). The question of just what caused this extinction is one that has fascinated scientists for many decades.

There does not seem to be a direct relationship between changes in climate and this extinction. For example, the extinctions in Australia occurred well before the last glacial maximum while those in Eurasia and the Americas happened much later. This suggests there is no direct climactic commonality between these extinctions. There are four principal theories about what happened, and each of these theories has its supporters and detractors, with valid arguments both for and against.

The human hunting hypothesis suggests that human hunters became increasingly adept at hunting large herbivores, to the extent that they notably decreased the population of these creatures in some areas. This in turn led to a shortage of prey for the carnivores that also hunted these creatures, which led to a decrease in carnivore populations. Eventually, the population decreases in both hunters and the hunted caused widespread mass extinctions.

There is some good circumstantial evidence to support the hypothesis that humans hunted large herbivores. For example, cave paintings have been discovered showing early *Homo sapiens* hunting large herbivores, bones of these creatures have been discovered with evidence of cut marks clearly caused by human tools, and in some places, the bones of large herbivores and humans have been found together.

Differences in biogeographical diversity also seem to support this hypothesis. In Africa, for example, where the earliest humans existed, there is currently a far greater diversity of species than in areas such as the Americas or Australia where humans arrived much later. Scientists who support the hunting hypothesis explain that this was because animals in Africa quickly learned to be wary of humans while animals in other areas were hunted to extinction before they became aware that humans posed a threat.

There also seems to be a correlation between the appearance of humans and mass extinctions. In Australia, for example, the wave of mass extinctions seems to have coincided with the first arrival of humans. This was the case in nearby Tasmania as well, although it happened later as humans did not colonize Tasmania until a few thousand years after arriving in mainland Australia. Broadly, the wave of extinctions seems to follow the spread of humans and was most severe where humans arrived later, giving the indigenous species less time to develop effective avoidance strategies.

Set against this evidence, there are a number of valid objections to the human hunting hypothesis. In most hunter-prey models, it is impossible for hunters to drive their prey to the point of extinction simply because as prey disappears, hunter populations also dwindle due to increased competition for a reducing food supply. In addition, while there is good archeological evidence that humans in, for example, North America hunted mammoth, mastodon and bison, there is no evidence that they hunted any other species. So, while this hunting could possibly account for the extinction of these species and the carnivores that preyed upon them, it does not account for the extinction of other species, such as camels. There is also some question about whether the relatively small number of humans could manage to hunt so efficiently that species were driven to extinction. Amongst other things, this would suggest the killing of animals far beyond what was required for food. Given the difficulty and danger of hunting these large creatures, this does seem unlikely. And there is the unexplained fact that some species that were certainly the target of human hunting in this period, such as bison, survived and even thrived until relatively recently.

There is a subsidiary theory closely related to the human hunting theory, called the second-order predation hypothesis. This postulates that, instead of humans hunting large herbivores to the point of extinction, they instead hunted the carnivores that preyed on these herbivores. This then caused overpopulation amongst the herbivores and the eventual exhaustion of the plant life needed to support these creatures.

However, there are problems with this theory too. The most notable is that most models suggest that, if the prey population increases, the population of hunters will also rise quickly and dramatically. It is very difficult to imagine early humans being able to completely eradicate completely large predators, such as saber-toothed cats. If they had reduced the population of these animals to the point where the population of natural prey increased, then the logical answer would be a corresponding increase in the saber-toothed cat population, not their complete extinction.

Overall, the human hunting hypothesis is an attractive way to explain the Late Pleistocene mass extinction, and there does seem to be a correlation in time between the arrival of humans and extinctions; however, there are some valid and important objections to this being the primary cause of the Late Pleistocene mass extinctions.

The hyperdisease hypothesis is a theory that asserts the Late Pleistocene Mass Extinction was caused indirectly by humans who brought with them some new form of virulent disease that killed large numbers of animals. This theory proposes that either humans themselves, or the domesticated animals they brought with them, carried some pathogen that infected large numbers of indigenous animals. This mainly affected larger animals because they were more susceptible to pathogens than smaller species which typically had a shorter gestation period and relatively larger populations.

For this theory to work, there must have been a highly lethal pathogen (a mortality rate of at least 75% has been suggested as necessary to account for the extinctions of whole populations) capable of infecting both sexes and all ages of a large number of species, but only used humans as a passive reservoir. If the pathogen had affected humans in the same way as other species, humans would have become extinct too.

However, just as with the human hunting theory, there are some fundamental flaws in the hyperdisease theory. The most significant is that the disease would have to have been capable of affecting a vast number of different species with a very high level of lethality. The most virulent of today's known pathogens, such as West Nile virus, are simply not capable of causing extinction nor infecting a broad range of species. The other issue is that this pathogen would have to be extremely selective. In North America, for example, it would have to have infected and wiped out the population of dire wolves while not affecting closely related species in the same area such as the Grey wolf. Similarly, it would have to have killed some species of goats and birds entirely while leaving others intact. The problem is, there is no known pathogen capable of this kind of selective infection.

One suggestion is that the disease, whatever it was, was carried by humans' domesticated animals rather than humans themselves, with dogs often being cited as the best candidates. However, not all extinctions support this. In Australia for example, the extinctions coincided with the arrival of humans; domesticated dogs did not arrive until 30,000 years later. While this theory sounds superficially attractive, it does not provide a complete answer.

Between around 15,000 and 10,000 years ago, Earth's climate was changing, with a gradual increase in global temperature as well as a decrease in ice sheets. One suggestion is that cold-adapted animals, such as the wooly mammoth and wooly rhinoceros, were simply unable to cope with this temperature and succumbed to heat stress, eventually leading to the complete extinction of these species.

The main argument against temperature alone being the main driver for extinction is that previous interglacial periods had been as warm (or in some cases, warmer) than the period that began 15,000 years ago, and species such as the mammoth had survived these with no alarming reduction in numbers. It is also notable that in some isolated areas free from human colonization (Wrangel Island in the Arctic Ocean, for example), wooly mammoth populations survived for much longer and well beyond the initial increase in temperature. This makes it unlikely that the temperature increase alone was responsible for these extinctions.

Another theory suggests that the overall increase in temperature brought more extreme weather including hotter summers and colder winters, and this in turn caused changes in the vegetation on which large herbivores relied. As the populations of large herbivores declined due to these changes in their food supply, the populations of their predators also declined.

However, just like the temperature theory, this theory has some flaws. Namely, such changes in weather and vegetation must have accompanied previous glacial and interglacial periods, but these did not bring about the mass extinctions seen in the Late Pleistocene. It is also notable that large animals are able to store more body fat than their smaller counterparts, and this generally makes then less susceptible to seasonal changes in food supply. With this in mind, the extinctions should have applied as much, if not more, to smaller species, and yet that was not the case. Virtually all the species that became extinct during this period were larger animals.

The Comet Hypothesis

The Comet Hypothesis (also known as the Younger Dryas impact hypothesis) suggests that somewhere between 12,800 and 11,700 years ago, the Earth was struck by fragments of a disintegrating comet or asteroid. Supporters of this theory believe that fragments impacted fifty different sites across Europe, Western Asia, North America and South America causing extensive burning that in turn caused abrupt climate change through an impact winter. This sudden climate change was responsible, it is claimed, for the mass extinctions during this time.

This theory was first mentioned as long ago as 1694 when astronomer Edmond Halley suggested that accounts of the Biblical flood might have been caused by the near-impact of a comet on Earth in the Late Pleistocene. However, this theory was generally discarded until it was revived in 2006 with the publication of a new book, *The Cycle of Cosmic Catastrophes: How a Stone-Age Comet Changed the Course of World Culture*, by Richard Firestone, Allen West and Simon Warwick-Smith. This book cited evidence of widespread impact fires and the existence of nanodiamonds (generally associated with bolide impacts) at a number of sites to support the theory of an asteroid or comet impact.

However, many scientists disagree with the evidence, claiming that supposed widespread impact fires is a misinterpretation of the evidence, and that the nanodiamonds and other evidence of impact either do not exist or are the result of a misinterpretation of effects of a terrestrial origin.

Overall, there does not seem to be any scientific consensus on what caused the LGP to end or what caused the Late Pleistocene mass extinction. While all the theories put forward have some merit, none seem to provide a complete answer. All we can be certain about is that something dramatic happened somewhere around 12,000 years ago that caused the extinction of a number of large species that had survived for hundreds of thousands of years.

In many cases, the extinction of these species seemed to coincide with the spread of humans, and in areas where humans colonized later or did not arrive, many species seem to have survived for longer. This strongly suggests a connection between the arrival of humans and this extinction, but so far no one has been able to convincingly explain how human activity could have directly caused these extinctions. Like so many other aspects of the Pleistocene Epoch, the precise causes of this extinction remain a mystery.

The End of the Pleistocene Epoch

In 1932, Edgar B. Howard, an archaeology research associate for the University of Pennsylvania Museum, made an astonishing discovery near the small town of Clovis, New Mexico. He heard that a work crew building a new road had discovered what seemed to be fossilized bones. When he investigated, he determined there were not only a number of bones, but a carefully crafted stone spearhead within the fossilized ribcage of a mammoth – a very significant discovery. It was the first time that conclusive evidence had been discovered showing humans had not only equipped themselves with stone tools and weapons, but also coexisted with creatures such as mammoths and saber-toothed cats in North America.

The people revealed by this find became known as the Clovis Culture, the first culture in North America and the oldest known culture in the Western Hemisphere. Subsequent finds confirmed that Clovis people were present in virtually all parts of North, Central and South America from around 13,000 years ago to 12,700 years ago. These people are significant because they provide us with a snapshot of human activity in the Late Pleistocene, before the mass extinctions and before the planet moved into the warmer weather of the Holocene.

Extensive study of Clovis Culture indicates an origin in Mongolia and Siberia as well as a link to later Amerindian nations. Genetic testing of modern Native American people further confirms this link with Siberia. In 2010, DNA testing was performed on the well-preserved bones of a one-year-old Clovis boy found near Anzick, Montana were DNA testing. Testing confirmed this boy was a descendent of people from Siberia and the ancestor of up to 80% of modern Native American people. Even the remains of the dogs of the Clovis people seem to confirm their place of origin – DNA testing shows these dogs are not related to North American wolves or dogs, but to an ancient Siberian breed of sled dog. So how did people from Siberia and Mongolia get to North America?

The answer to this question lies in the much lower sea levels during the LGP. So much water was locked up in ice sheets that sea levels were as much as four hundred feet below today's levels. This led to the formation of the Bering Land Bridge, an area of steppe that linked eastern Siberia with present-day Alaska. Research suggests these people migrated from Siberia to America via this land bridge around 13,000 years ago, and this seems to be confirmed by genetic testing. When global temperatures began to rise, sea levels also rose as the ice melted, submerging the land bridge and cutting off the route for the people who had migrated to America from Siberia.

What remains a mystery is how these people colonized the new continent so quickly and developed distinct new tools and weapons that were never seen in Siberia.

Archeological discoveries suggest the Clovis people had a significant presence for only around three hundred years, but in that short time, they somehow spread from present-day Alaska south to North, Central and even South America. Clovis people were not the first humans to arrive in America – there is evidence of human activity thousands of years before these people arrived; however, their distinct culture had a major impact on the development of human societies in the Americas.

One of the most distinctive artifacts left by this culture is what has become known as the *Clovis point*, which are spearheads of a unique design. Most are chipped from chert, obsidian or other types of brittle, easily flaked stone and all feature the same basic shape – an extremely sharp point and blades featuring grooves, or "flutes", that make the tip lighter while retaining its strength and still fit easily into a wooden shaft. These spearpoints are very distinctive and seem to belong exclusively to the Clovis culture. None have been in found in Siberia where these people are thought to have originated, and none have been discovered after the end of this culture. It seems these beautifully made weapons were invented by these people after they arrived in America and the secret of their creation was lost when this culture ended.

These spear tips are so distinctive that they have been used to identify centers of Clovis culture in the Americas. Over ten thousand "Clovis points" have been found in fifteen hundred locations across North America and as far south as Venezuela. The oldest Clovis points were found in Texas and have been dated to around 13,500 years ago. Within a few centuries, they had spread across the continent. A genetic study in 2017 discovered that people from Belize, Brazil, the Central Andes and southern South America had DNA that linked them to Siberian ancestors and many had genetic commonalities with the Clovis people.

Archeologists have taken these discoveries to mean that this culture spread across the continent in an incredibly short period of time. It has been said that no other culture has dominated America so quickly or so completely. But just who were these people?

Initially, it was assumed that Clovis people were hunter-gatherers who specialized in hunting Pleistocene megafauna, mammoths, mastodons and other large herbivores. Many museums featured dramatic dioramas with groups of Clovis hunters working together to bring down a mammoth or escape from a saber-toothed cat. However, more recent studies suggest that this was a much more complex culture.

While it certainly possible that Clovis hunters tackled large animals such as mammoths, it now seems likely that this was no more than an occasional (and high risk) activity. Study of a large number of Clovis sites found less than twenty examples of the bones of large herbivores killed by hunting. It seems much more likely that these people foraged for edible plants and berries, fished and more often hunted smaller mammals.

In addition to Clovis points, other discoveries at Clovis sites have produced many additional stone artifacts, including carefully-crated scrapers, drills blades and even fine stone needles. The discoveries made so far have all been of bone or stone items with a few ivory pieces. It is very likely that Clovis people also made clothing, blankets and some sort of shelters using animal skins, as well as baskets and other containers, but nothing remains of these so archeologists have been forced to speculate about just what the Clovis lifestyle looked like.

It seems very likely that these were bands of nomadic hunter-gatherers, generally of between twenty-five to fifty people, following game and taking advantage of the availability of nuts, berries and other naturally occurring plant foods. Anthropologists don't know whether these bands regarded themselves as part of a larger Clovis tribe or as separate entities, though the sharing of technology seen in the Clovis points strongly suggests there was some sort of communication between bands.

Most Clovis camps discovered to date are near the sea or close to rivers or lakes, suggesting that these people were also fishermen. One Clovis campsite even provides evidence of the digging of a well – the first known example of human attempts to control the water supply. Only one Clovis burial site has been discovered to date – that of the one-year-old boy discovered in Anzick, New Mexico. This grave also included stone tools and fragments that seemed to have been arranged in a ritual manner, suggesting that burial was an important event for these people.

However, it wasn't just their dead that the Clovis people buried. A number of Clovis "cache sites" have also been discovered where collections of spear-points, blades and other stone tools appear to have been intentionally buried. No one is certain why this would have been done, though these would have been significant items and likely that either whoever buried these items intended to return for them later or that these burials were part of some kind of ritual.

Just like so many aspects of the Pleistocene, what happened to the Clovis people is a mystery. They emerged as a culture, colonized large areas of the New World and then, after just a few hundred years, this culture vanished. No Clovis artifacts have been found that date to later than around 12,700 years ago. Many subsequent cultures emerged in the Americas, including the Folsom, Gainey, Suwannee-Simpson, Plainview-Goshen, Cumberland and Redstone. DNA confirms that the people of these later cultures derived from the Clovis people, but the Clovis culture itself seemed to vanish completely – no "Clovis points", for example, have been discovered amongst the artifacts left by these later cultures.

The abrupt disappearance of the Clovis culture happened at the same time as the mass-extinction event that killed so many large mammals in the same area, which has inevitably given rise to speculation that the two events were linked, though it is difficult to assess precisely how.

The Clovis people certainly did hunt mammoth, but even if mammoths had become extinct there would have been lots of other game for hunters to pursue so it is unlikely that this could have led to the end of the Clovis culture. Conversely, it is difficult to imagine that the Clovis people were so numerous and so efficient that they could have hunted a large number of species to the point of complete extinction. It is also notable that similar extinctions happened in other parts of the world where there were no Clovis people.

All we can say with confidence is that mammoths, mastodons, saber-toothed cats and many other species disappeared at around the same time that the Clovis culture ended. It seems too much to accept that this was coincidence, and is more likely that whatever caused the late Pleistocene megafauna mass extinctions somehow also led to the end of Clovis culture.

However, the Clovis culture is important not just because it is the antecedent of virtually all North American cultures that followed, but because it tells us so much about human society in the Pleistocene. Clovis finds make it clear that these were not the brutish cavemen previously imagined. They were capable of creating artifacts of great beauty and effective functionality and of communicating the knowledge required to produce these to other members of the tribe. The few burial sites discovered to date suggest that they had rituals and may have had sophisticated belief systems. The Clovis culture is important not just in explaining subsequent culture in America, but it also enables scientists to deduce what was happening in other parts of the world as well. The Clovis culture provides a snapshot of human life in the Pleistocene and of the kind of society from which all subsequent cultures developed.

The end of the Clovis culture also marks the end of the Pleistocene Epoch and the beginning of the Holocene, the epoch in which we live today. The Clovis people existed in a world of glaciers and ice sheets populated by mammoths and mastodons. Soon the glaciers would begin to retreat, temperatures would begin to rise and the Mammoths and many other creatures would vanish completely.

The Holocene brought a new world, increasingly free of ice, but missing many of the species that had populated Earth for thousands of years. Modern societies are still living with the legacy of the Pleistocene, both in terms of the global climate and the flora and fauna that populate our planet. In many parts of the world, the legacy of the Clovis culture lives on in terms of genetic inheritance.

Conclusion

The beginning of the Pleistocene Epoch was over two and a half mya, an unimaginably long stretch of time in human terms. However, its end was less than twelve thousand years ago, a mere heartbeat in terms of the history of our planet. People still live in a landscape shaped by the Pleistocene and the development of *Homo sapiens* was directly influenced by the advancing and retreating ice of that period.

Despite all that is known about the Pleistocene, many mysteries still remain. The waves of climate change that characterized the Pleistocene may be very important as scientists continue to struggle to fully understand the impact of human activity on climate. However, there is still no complete agreement on just what the mechanisms were that caused glaciers to form, advance and then retreat and melt or whether the Earth may yet face another glacial period.

In human terms, there is also much we can learn from this period. The Clovis people and their contemporaries are our close ancestors, yet we know relatively little about how they lived and nothing at all about why this culture came to an abrupt end after just a few hundred years. In terms of the animals of this period, we know much more than we do about creatures from the more distant past. All that we know about dinosaurs, for example, must be deduced from a few dusty, fossilized bones. For the mammoth, for example, we know much more. Mammoth carcasses deep frozen in Siberia tell us not only what these creatures looked like in life, but some have even showed what they ate as a last meal. A few have provided blood samples, leading to hopes that it might even be possible to clone new mammoths, though it is by no means certain that this is possible.

Even with all of this information available, we still don't know why mammoths and so many other large animals of the Late Pleistocene suddenly became extinct at around the same time that humans began colonizing the Earth. Was there a connection between these two events? It seems beyond coincidence and yet scientists have so far been unable to explain how the arrival of a relatively small number of humans could cause such widespread extinction amongst large animals.

In some ways, the Pleistocene Epoch is one of the best-known of all the prehistoric periods of Earth, but the knowledge we have also throws into stark contrast the mysteries that remain. Researchers know a great deal about what happened in the Pleistocene, but they remain largely ignorant of why and how, meaning the Pleistocene is at the same time one of the best and least-understood of Earth's many eras.

Online Resources

<u>Other books about ancient history by Charles River Editors</u>

<u>Other books about the Pleistocene on Amazon</u>

Further Reading

Amthor, J. E.; Grotzinger, John P.; Schröder, Stefan; Bowring, Samuel A.; Ramezani, Jahandar; Martin, Mark W.; Matter, Albert (2003). "Extinction of Cloudina and Namacalathus at the Precambrian-Cambrian boundary in Oman". Geology. 31 (5): 431–434. Bibcode:2003Geo....31..431A. doi:10.1130/0091-7613(2003)031<0431:EOCANA>2.0.CO;2.

Collette, J. H.; Gass, K. C.; Hagadorn, J. W. (2012). "Protichnites eremita unshelled? Experimental model-based neoichnology and new evidence for a euthycarcinoid affinity for this ichnospecies". Journal of Paleontology. 86 (3): 442–454. doi:10.1666/11-056.1. S2CID

129234373.

Collette, J. H.; Hagadorn, J. W. (2010). "Three-dimensionally preserved arthropods from Cambrian Lagerstatten of Quebec and Wisconsin". Journal of Paleontology. 84 (4): 646–667. doi:10.1666/09-075.1. S2CID 130064618.

Getty, P. R.; Hagadorn, J. W. (2008). "Reinterpretation of Climactichnites Logan 1860 to include subsurface burrows, and erection of Musculopodus for resting traces of the trailmaker". Journal of Paleontology. 82 (6): 1161–1172. doi:10.1666/08-004.1. S2CID 129732925.

Gould, S. J. (1989). Wonderful Life: the Burgess Shale and the Nature of Life. New York: Norton.

Ogg, J. (June 2004). "Overview of Global Boundary Stratotype Sections and Points (GSSPs)". Archived from the original on 23 April 2006. Retrieved 30 April 2006.

Owen, R. (1852). "Description of the impressions and footprints of the Protichnites from the Potsdam sandstone of Canada". Geological Society of London Quarterly Journal. 8 (1–2): 214–225. doi:10.1144/GSL.JGS.1852.008.01-02.26. S2CID 130712914.

Peng, S.; Babcock, L.E.; Cooper, R.A. (2012). "The Cambrian Period" (PDF). The Geologic Time Scale.

Schieber, J.; Bose, P. K.; Eriksson, P. G.; Banerjee, S.; Sarkar, S.; Altermann, W.; Catuneau, O. (2007). Atlas of Microbial Mat Features Preserved within the Clastic Rock Record. Elsevier. pp. 53–71.

Yochelson, E. L.; Fedonkin, M. A. (1993). "Paleobiology of Climactichnites, and Enigmatic Late Cambrian Fossil". Smithsonian Contributions to Paleobiology. 74 (74): 1–74.

Free Books by Charles River Editors

We have brand new titles available for free most days of the week. To see which of our titles are currently free, click on this link.

Discounted Books by Charles River Editors

We have titles at a discount price of just 99 cents everyday. To see which of our titles are currently 99 cents, click on this link.